Primary Sources *of* American Symbols™

The Bald Eagle

Jennifer Silate

The Rosen Publishing Group's
PowerKids Press™
PRIMARY SOURCE

Published in 2006 by The Rosen Publishing Group, Inc.
29 East 21st Street, New York, NY 10010

Editor: Eric Fein
Book Design: Michael DeLisio
Photo Researcher: Sherri Liberman

Photo Credits: Cover, pp. 1, 3 © EyeWire, Inc.; pp. 4 (left), 7 (left) National Archives and Records Administration Record Group 360; p. 4 (right) © The Corcoran Gallery of Art/Corbis; p. 7 (right) Independence National Historical Park; p. 8 (left) Natural History Museum, London, UK/Bridgeman Art Library; p. 8 (right) courtesy of The American Numismatic Society © 2002. All rights reserved; p. 11 (left) Library of Congress Manuscript Division; p. 11 (right) © Academy of Natural Sciences of Philadelphia/Corbis; p. 12 (right) Reproduced from the original held by the Department of Special Collections of the University Libraries of Notre Dame; p. 15 (left) Library of Congress Rare Book and Special Collection Division; p. 15 (right) Picture History; p. 16 (left) © Joseph Sohm; Visions of America/Corbis; p. 16 (right) © Swim Ink/Corbis; p. 19 © OSF/Lon Lauber/Animals Animals/ Earth Scenes; p. 20 © AP/Wide World Photos

First Edition

Library of Congress Cataloging-in-Publication Data

Silate, Jennifer.
    The bald eagle / Jennifer Silate.— 1st ed.
        p. cm. — (Primary sources of American symbols)
    Includes index.
    Contents: Creating an official seal — Choosing a national symbol — Why a bald eagle?
Franklin's turkey — Coins and money — Old Abe —Bald eagles as symbols — Threats
to America's symbol — Eagles on the rise — Timeline.
    ISBN 1-4042-2697-4 (lib. bdg.)
    1. United States—Seal—Juvenile literature. 2. Bald eagle—United States—Juvenile
literature. 3. Emblems, National—United States—Juvenile literature. 4. Animals—
Symbolic aspects—Juvenile literature. 5. Signs and symbols—United States—Juvenile
literature. [1. United States—Seal. 2. Bald eagle. 3. Eagles. 4. Emblems, National. 5.
Signs and symbols.] I. Title. II. Series: Silate, Jennifer. Primary sources of American
symbols.

CD5610.S55 2006
929.9'2'0973—dc22

                                                                        2003026823

Manufactured in the United States of America

Contents

1 Creating an Official Seal   5

2 Choosing a National Symbol   6

3 Why a Bald Eagle?   9

4 Franklin's Turkey   10

5 Coins and Money   13

6 Old Abe   14

7 Bald Eagles as Symbols   17

8 Threats to America's Symbol   18

9 Eagles on the Rise   21

Timeline   22

Glossary   23

Index   24

Web Sites   24

Primary Sources   24

Three different committees worked on designs for the official seal. This design was created by the second committee in 1780, and was not accepted.

Creating an Official Seal

The bald eagle has been an important **symbol** of the United States for more than 200 years. During the **American Revolutionary War**, colonial leaders **declared** America's independence from England. The leaders wanted to have a seal to use on official government papers.

In 1776, the **Continental Congress** formed a **committee** to create an official seal. Benjamin Franklin, Thomas Jefferson, and John Adams were on this first committee. Several **designs** for the seal, some featuring eagles, were considered. However, the committee was not satisfied with any of these designs.

Finally, in 1882, a third committee agreed to a design. Secretary of Congress Charles Thomson created this design, which used a bald eagle.

Benjamin Franklin (1706–1790) was on the first committee established to create an official seal. In his lifetime, Franklin was a famous printer and publisher, author, inventor and scientist, and politician.

Choosing a National Symbol

Charles Thomson's eagle held an olive branch in one claw. In the other claw was a bundle of arrows. The olive branch stood for peace and the arrows stood for war. In Thomson's drawing, the eagle is looking at the olive branch. This showed that America was in favor of peace. Thomson's design was very popular with the members of Congress. His design was approved on June 20, 1782. The seal was named the Great Seal of the United States. The bald eagle quickly became well known as a symbol of America. In 1787, the bald eagle became the official national symbol of America.

Charles Thomson's design for an official seal for the new American nation was approved on June 20, 1782. Thomson used elements from previous designs.

Charles Thomson (1729-1824) was secretary of the First Continental Congress from 1774 to 1789. He not only kept records of the activities of the congress, but also recorded the history of the American Revolutionary War.

E PLURIBUS UNUM

Over the years, the bald eagle has been the subject of many works of art. This eighteenth-century painting is by artist Mark Catesby.

Why a Bald Eagle?

The bald eagle was chosen to be the national symbol of the United States for several reasons. Native Americans believed the bald eagle was a symbol of strength. Also, during the Revolutionary War, bald eagles had flown over a battlefield. The eagles became symbols of the fight for freedom. The bald eagle is also found only in North America, making it truly an American bird.

The bald eagle is large and powerful. It lives many years. Because of these features, many Americans liked the bald eagle as a symbol for the new country. These people hoped that America would grow to become a strong, powerful nation.

In 1793, the U.S. government made this Indian peace medal, featuring a bald eagle. Peace medals were given to Native American tribes as a sign of friendship.

Franklin's Turkey

Not everyone wanted the bald eagle to be America's national symbol. Benjamin Franklin did not think the bald eagle was a good choice. Bald eagles often steal fish from other birds. Franklin thought that this was a sign of laziness. When they are chased by smaller birds, bald eagles will sometimes flee. Franklin thought this made the bald eagle appear cowardly. Franklin suggested that the turkey be used as the national symbol. A turkey fights off animals that come near it. Franklin believed that this would make it a good symbol for the United States. Franklin's idea did not become very popular. The bald eagle remained the national symbol of the United States.

Benjamin Franklin thought that the turkey would make a better national symbol than the bald eagle. This painting of a wild turkey is by John J. Audubon. It was made in about 1830.

...too much like a Turkey, or Turky. For my own part I wish the Bald Eagle had not been chosen as the Representative of our Country. He is a Bird of bad moral Character. He does not get his Living honestly. You may have seen him perch'd on some dead Tree near the River, where, too lazy to fish for himself, he watches the Labour of the Fishing Hawk; and when that diligent Bird has at length taken a Fish, and is bearing it to his Nest for the Support of his Mate and young Ones, the Bald Eagle pursues him & takes it from him. With all this Injustice, he is never in good Case but like those among Men who live by Sharping & Robbing he is generally poor and often very lousy. Besides he is a rank Coward: The little King Bird not bigger than a Sparrow attacks him boldly & drives him out of the District. He is therefore by no means a proper Emblem for the brave and honest Cincinnati of America who have driven all the King birds from our Country, tho' exactly fit for that Order of Knights which the French call Chevaliers d'Industrie. I am on this account...

In this letter to his daughter, Franklin explains why he does not like the idea of the bald eagle being the national symbol. Franklin writes, "He is a bird of bad moral character. He does not get his living honestly."

The back of a $1 bill shows a bald eagle holding a ribbon in its beak with the Latin words, "E Pluribus Unum." These words mean "Out of many, one."

Coins and Money

One of the most common ways that the bald eagle is used to represent America is by placing its likeness on money. In fact, the bald eagle was used on American coins even *before* it became the national symbol. The earliest known use of the bald eagle on American money was on a coin made in Massachusetts in 1776.

In 1795, the bald eagle appeared on a 10-dollar gold coin. Since then, the bald eagle has been used on many other coins and bills. The quarter, half dollar, and the dollar bill all have a picture of an eagle on them. In fact, most of today's American money has an eagle pictured on it.

Massachusetts Coppers were half-cent and one-cent coins made by the Massachusetts government in 1787 and 1788. This Massachusetts Copper is from 1788.

Old Abe

During the **American Civil War**, a live bald eagle became an important symbol of the United States of America. This eagle was the **mascot** for a **regiment** in the Northern army. He was called Old Abe, named after President Abraham Lincoln. Old Abe traveled more than 14,000 miles with his regiment. He was at 37 battles. Old Abe served as a symbol of the United States and freedom for the Union soldiers. After the Civil War, Old Abe lived in the capitol building in Madison, Wisconsin. When he died, Old Abe was stuffed and put on display for people to see.

Old Abe became so popular during the Civil War that songs were written about him. Shown here is the sheet music to "We'll Sing to Abe Our Song!" from about 1865.

After he died, Old Abe was stuffed and displayed in the capitol building in Madison, Wisconsin. Legends say that during a battle, Old Abe would fly above the troops and screech loudly.

The *Seal of the President of the United States* also uses the bald eagle as a symbol. At one time, the head of the eagle on the presidential seal was turned toward the arrows the eagle holds in his claw.

Bald Eagles as Symbols

The **image** of the bald eagle has been used for many different purposes. Twelve states use an image of the bald eagle in their state seal. The bald eagle is also shown on the presidential seal. The bald eagle is pictured on many different postage stamps, too.

The bald eagle is not used as a symbol only by the government. Many businesses use the bald eagle in their **logos**. Many people have made works of art to honor the bald eagle. There are many poems, paintings, and **sculptures** in recognition of the bald eagle. A live bald eagle is sometimes flown at important events. The bald eagle reminds Americans of their freedom and the strength of the nation.

◀ *A bald eagle is used on this poster from World War I. The poster was used to remind people of the important work being done by the U.S. army.*

Threats to America's Symbol

The United States had come close to losing all of its living bald eagles. Some people had been shooting and killing bald eagles to keep them away from their livestock. In 1940, Congress passed a law that made it illegal to kill, buy, sell, or own a bald eagle. Congress wanted to keep the bald eagle alive and free to live where it wanted. Not long after Congress passed this law, farmers started using a chemical called **DDT** to kill insects. DDT washed off into the rivers and streams. Bald eagles ate fish that had DDT in them. The DDT made the bald eagles' eggs very thin. This caused the eggshells to break before the baby eagles could **hatch**. This resulted in the deaths of many baby bald eagles. By 1960, there were only about 900 bald eagles left in America.

This photo shows an eagle returning to its mate with a fish. Over time, the number of bald eagles in North America was greatly reduced by hunting and poisoned food supplies.

Challenger lands on his trainer's arm before the start of a Major League Baseball game in 2003.

Eagles on the Rise

Most uses of DDT were banned in 1972. Since then, people have been working to increase the number of bald eagles in the wild. While bald eagles are still **endangered**, their number is growing. Today, more than 55,000 bald eagles live in North America.

The bald eagle became an even more important symbol to America after the terrorist attacks on September 11, 2001. Baseball's World Series was held shortly after the attacks. A bald eagle named Challenger was released before the games began. Challenger's flight reminded everyone that although the country had been attacked, America's strength and freedom still **soared**.

Many efforts are being made to make sure that the American bald eagle survives. Here, an injured eagle is being recovered so that it can be taken for medical treatment.

Timeline

1776	America declares its independence from England. A committee is formed to create an official seal of the United States. The bald eagle is also used on a coin for the first time.
1782	Charles Thomson's design is approved as the Great Seal of the United States.
1787	The bald eagle becomes the national symbol.
1795	The bald eagle is put on a 10-dollar gold coin.
1861–1865	The American Civil War is fought.
1940	Congress passes a law making it illegal to buy, sell, own, or kill a bald eagle.
1960	The number of bald eagles in the wild drops to around 900.
1972	After it leads to the death of many bald eagles, most uses of DDT are banned.
1970s–1990s	Number of bald eagles in America increases.
2001	September 11 terrorist attacks take place. During baseball's 2001 World Series, a bald eagle named Challenger flies before the start of the games.

Glossary

American Civil War (uh-MER-uh-kuhn SIV-il WOR) The U.S. war between the Confederacy, or Southern states, and the Union, or Northern states, that lasted from 1861–1865.

American Revolutionary War (uh-MER-uh-kuhn rev-uh-LOO-shuh-ner-ee WOR) The war from 1775–1783 during which the American colonies fought against England. As a result, the United States of America was created.

committee (kuh-MIT-ee) A group of people chosen to discuss things and make decisions for a larger group.

Continental Congress (KON-tuh-nuhnt-el KON-gress) A group of people picked to decide laws for the American colonies

DDT (DEE-dee-tee) A chemical used to kill insects that also killed many bald eagles.

declared (di-KLAIR-id) To have announced something formally.

designs (di-ZINEZ) Drawings of things that can be built or made; the shapes or styles of things.

endangered (en-DAYN-jur-id) To put in a dangerous situation; in danger of becoming extinct.

hatch (HACH) When a baby bird breaks out of its egg.

image (IM-ij) A representation, such as a picture or a statue.

logos (LOH-gohz) Symbols that represent a particular company or organization.

mascot (MASS-kot) Something that is supposed to bring good luck, especially an animal kept by a sports team.

regiment (REJ-uh-muhnt) A military unit.

sculptures (SKUHLP-churz) Things that are carved or shaped out of stone, metal, marble, or clay, or cast in bronze or another metal.

soared (SOR-id) To have flown very high in the air.

symbol (SIM-buhl) A design or an object that represents something else.

Index

A
Adams, John, 5
American Civil War, 14
American Revolutionary War, 5
attacks, 21

C
Challenger, 21
committee, 5
Continental Congress, 5

D
DDT, 18, 21
declared, 5
designs, 5

E
endangered, 21

F
Franklin, Benjamin, 5, 10

G
government, 5, 17
Great Seal of the United States, 6

H
hatch, 18

I
image, 17
independence, 5·

J
Jefferson, Thomas, 5

L
Lincoln, Abraham, 14
livestock, 18
logos, 17

M
mascot, 14
money, 13

N
Native Americans, 9

O
Old Abe, 14
olive branch, 6

R
regiment, 14

S
sculptures, 17
seal, 5–6
soared, 21
strength, 9, 17, 21
symbol, 5–6, 9–10, 13–14, 17, 21

T
terrorist, 21
Thomson, Charles, 5–6

W
World Series, 21

Primary Sources

Cover: The American bald eagle. **Page 4 (left):** Second Committee, 1780: Hopkinson's drawings of his revised proposals from the Papers of the Continental Congress. U.S. National Archives and Records Administration (NARA). **(right):** Painting, *Benjamin Franklin* by Joseph Wright [1782]. **Page 7 (left)** George Thomson's design for the Great Seal of the United States [1782]. 099999NARA. **(right)** Charles Thomson, Secretary of Congress. Oil portrait by Charles Willson Peale [date unknown]. Independence National Historic Park. **Page 8 (left):** Aquila capite albo (white-headed eagle or bald eagle). Plate 1 from Volume 1 of National History of Carolina, Florida and the Bahamas. Colored engraving (c. eighteenth century). National History Museum, London, England. **(right):** Indian peace medal [1793]. American Numismatic Society, New York. **Page 11:** Wild turkey. Oil painting by John J. Audubon [c. 183]. Academy of Natural Sciences of Philadelphia. **(inset):** Letter by Benjamin Franklin to his daughter [1784]. Library of Congress. **Page 12:** One-dollar bill. **(right):** Massachusetts Copper [1788]. Notre Dame Libraries-Special Collections. **Page 15 (left):** "We'll Sing Our Song to Abe!": Sheet music about Lincoln, Emancipation, and the Civil War from the Alfred Whital Stern Collection of Lincolniana [c. 1865]. Library of Congress. **(right):** Old Abe the Battle Eagle. Photographic print [1876]. **Page 16 (left):** Seal of the President of the United States. **(right):** Poster, U.S. Army, At Home Abroad by Tom Woodburn [c. 1918]. **Page 19:** Bald eagle returning to mate in nest with fish. **Page 20 (left):** Challenger, an American bald eagle, and his trainer at a Major League Baseball game [2003]. **(right):** Two-year-old bald eagle at the DeSoto National Wildlife Refuge, Missouri Valley, Iowa [2002].

Web Sites

Due to the changing nature of Internet links, PowerKids Press has developed an on-line list of Web sites related to the subject of this book. This site is updated regularly. Please use this link to access the list:
www.powerkidslinks.com/psas/tbe